On May 26, 1978, I attended Frank Sinatra's
last appearance at the Latin Casino in Cherry Hill NJ.
Seated near the stage, I shot one roll of ASA 400 black
and white film. It took about 25 minutes from start to finish.
Sometime that summer, my friend Susan Rose developed
the film and printed the photographs.

For almost 38 years, these photos have been in file folders,
in drawers, and for the past eight years, in my garage.

Remarkably they have survived.

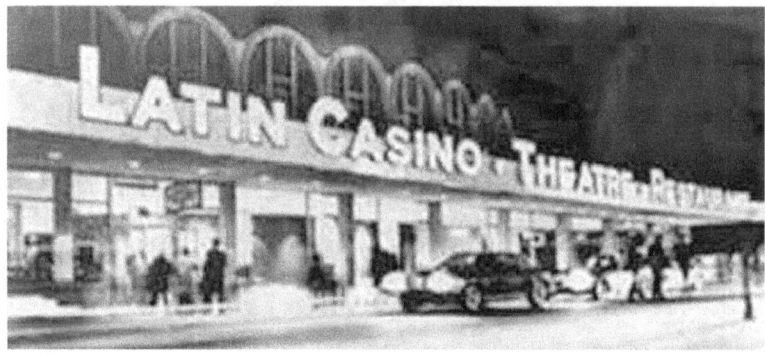

The Latin Casino first opened in 1948 at 1309 Walnut

Street in Philadelphia. In 1960, it was relocated to Cherry

Hill, NJ on Route 70 across from the Garden State

Racetrack. Until it closed in 1978, the plush 1,500-seat,

Vegas-style dinner theater was one of the great nightclubs

of its era, featuring a showcase of top entertainment.

An Evening with Frank

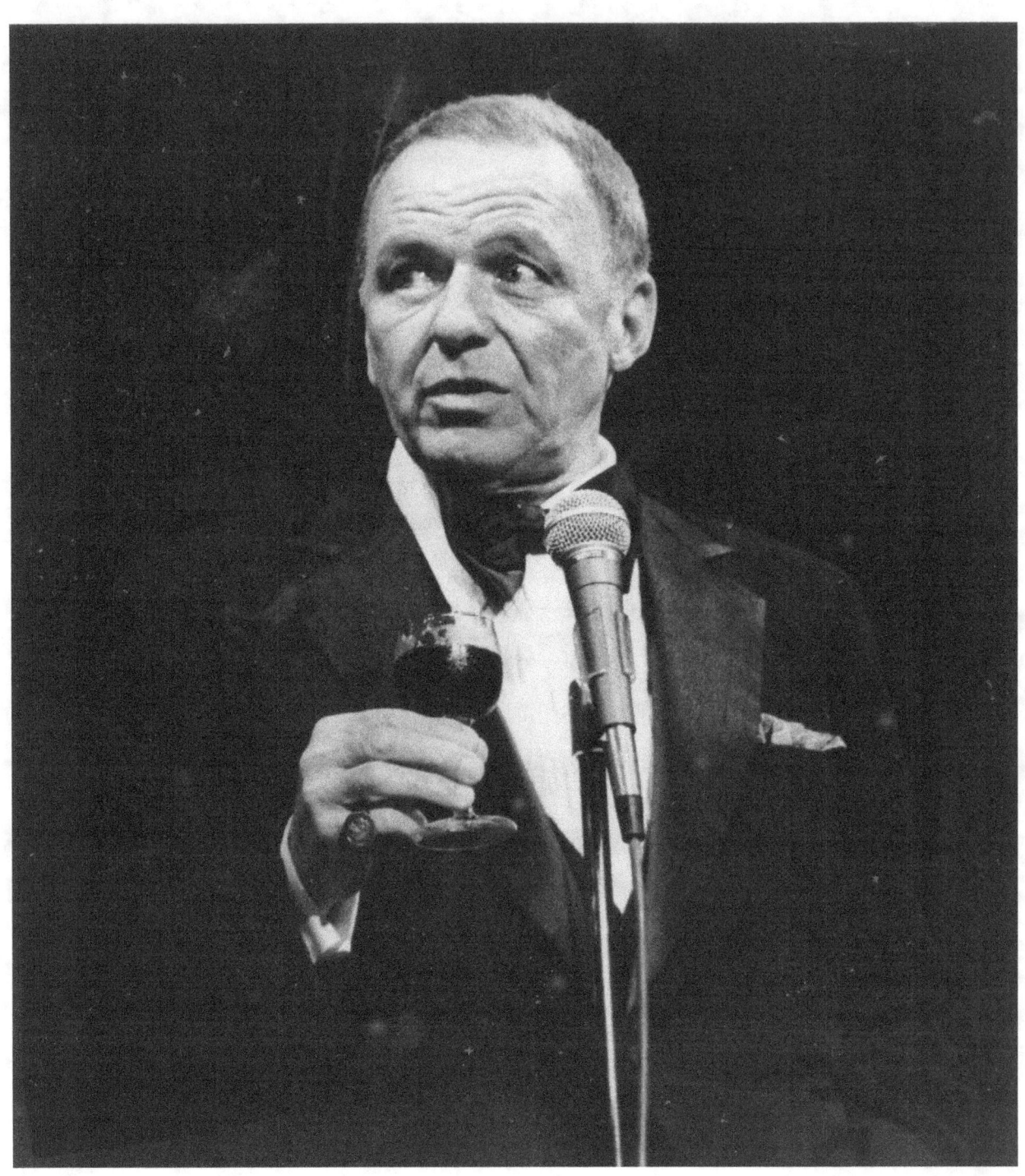

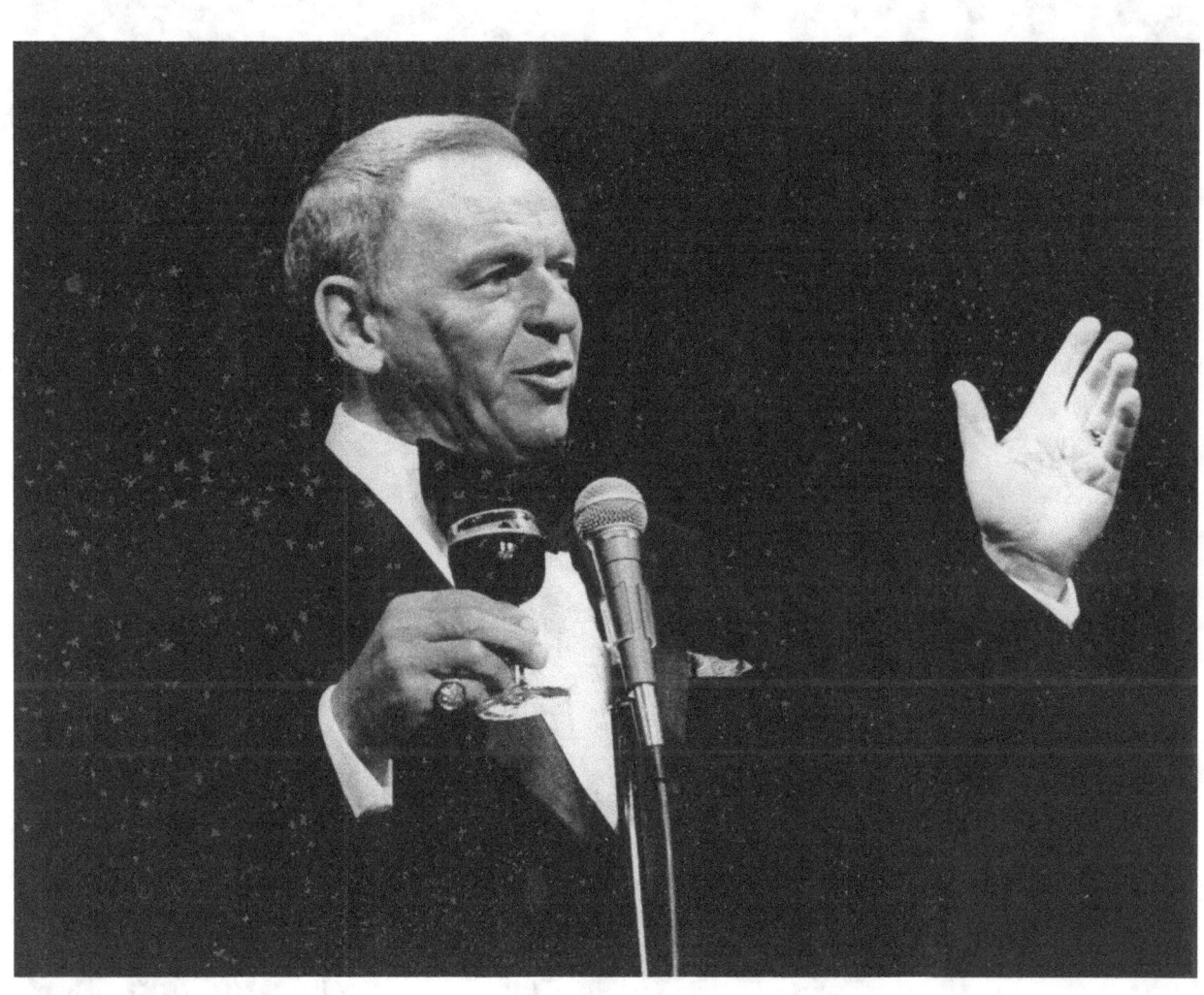

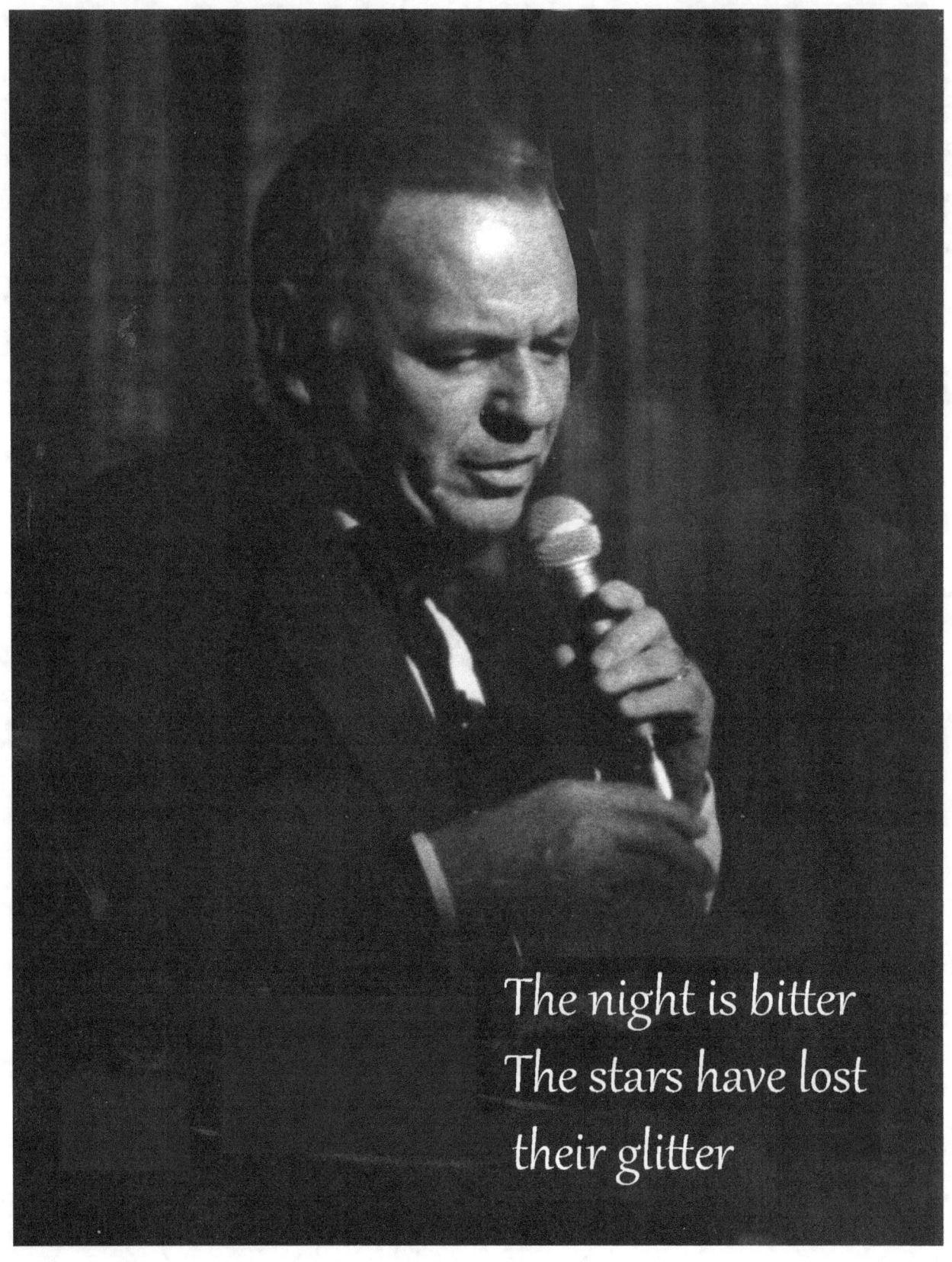

The night is bitter
The stars have lost
their glitter

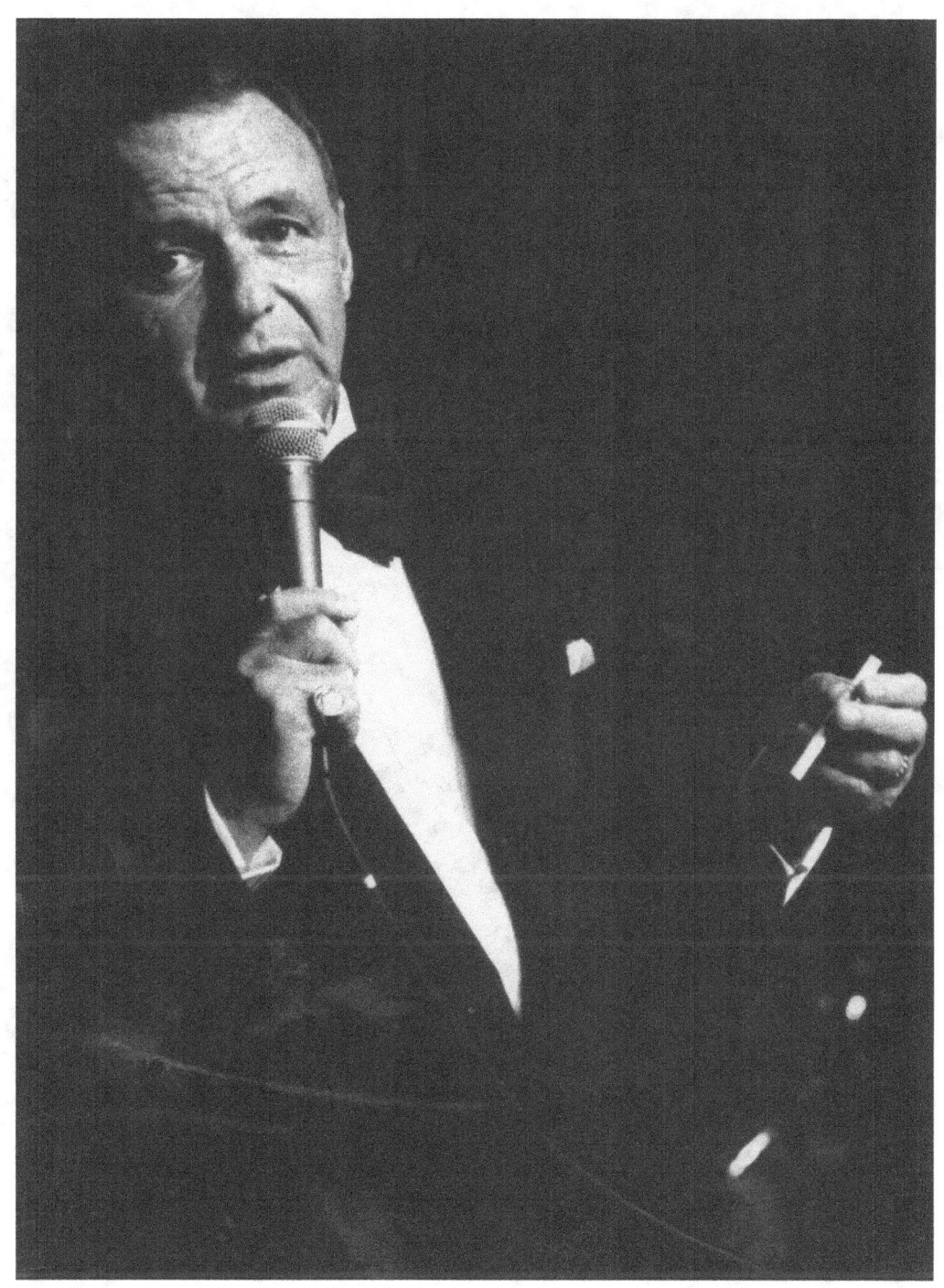

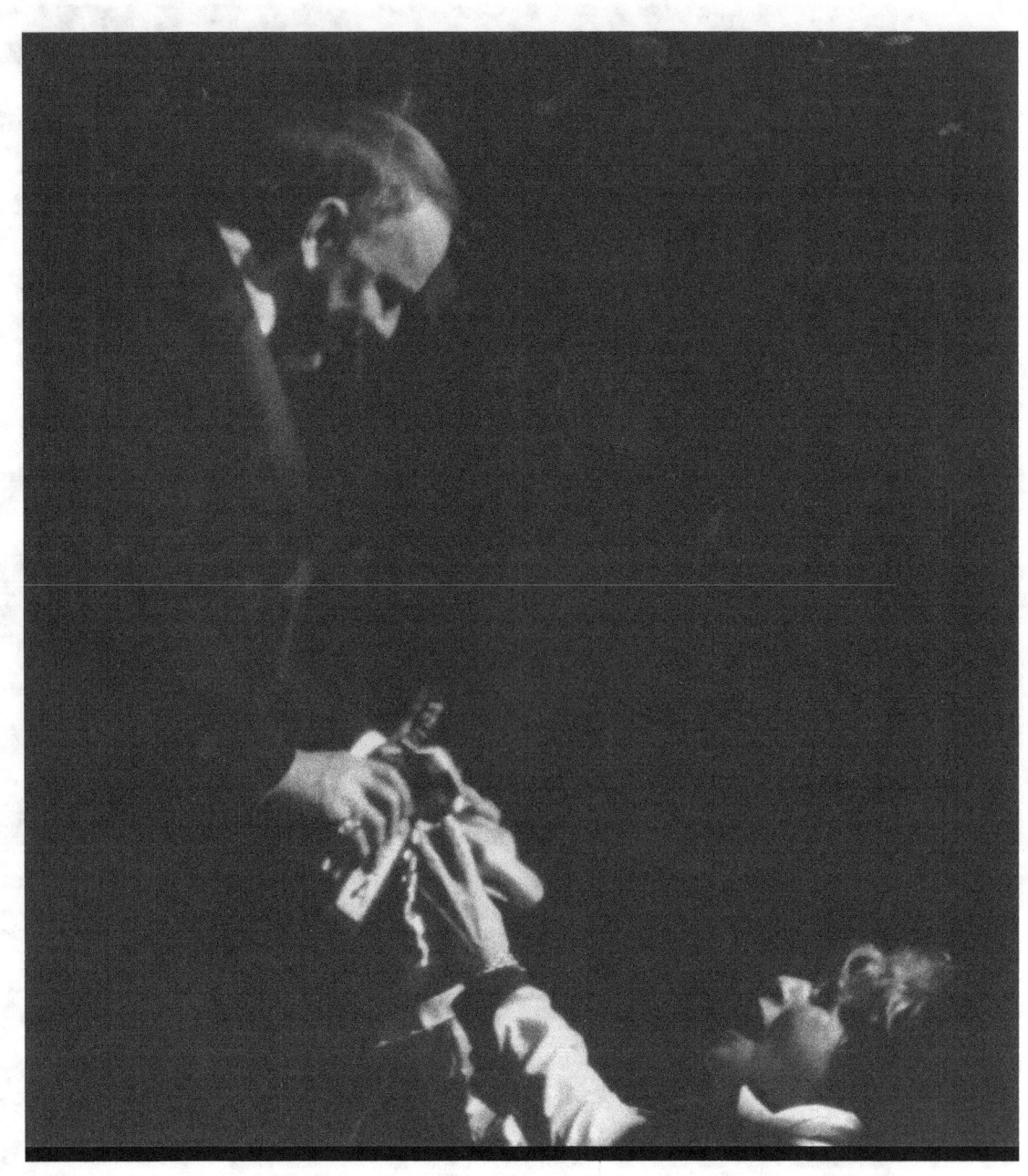

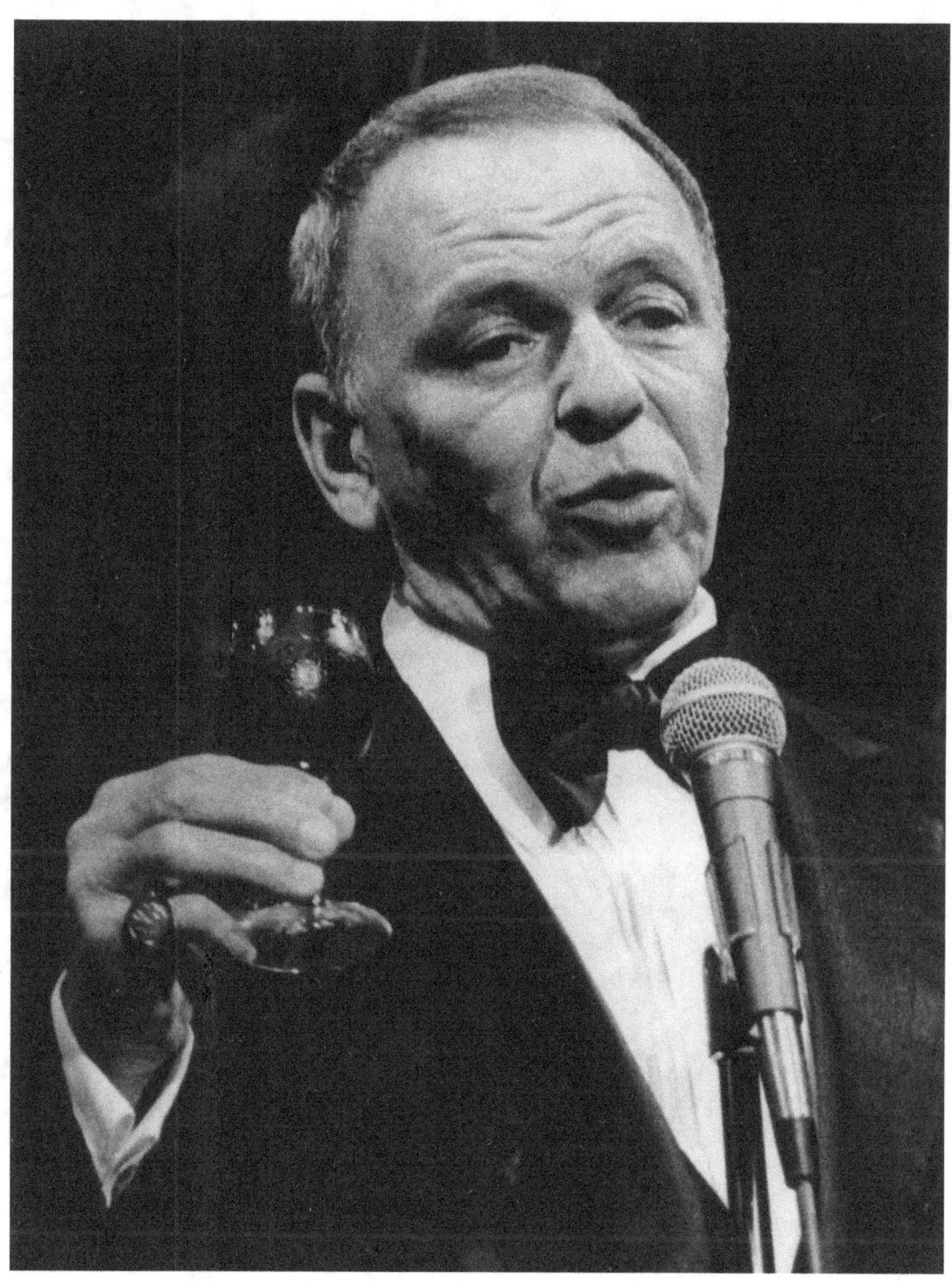

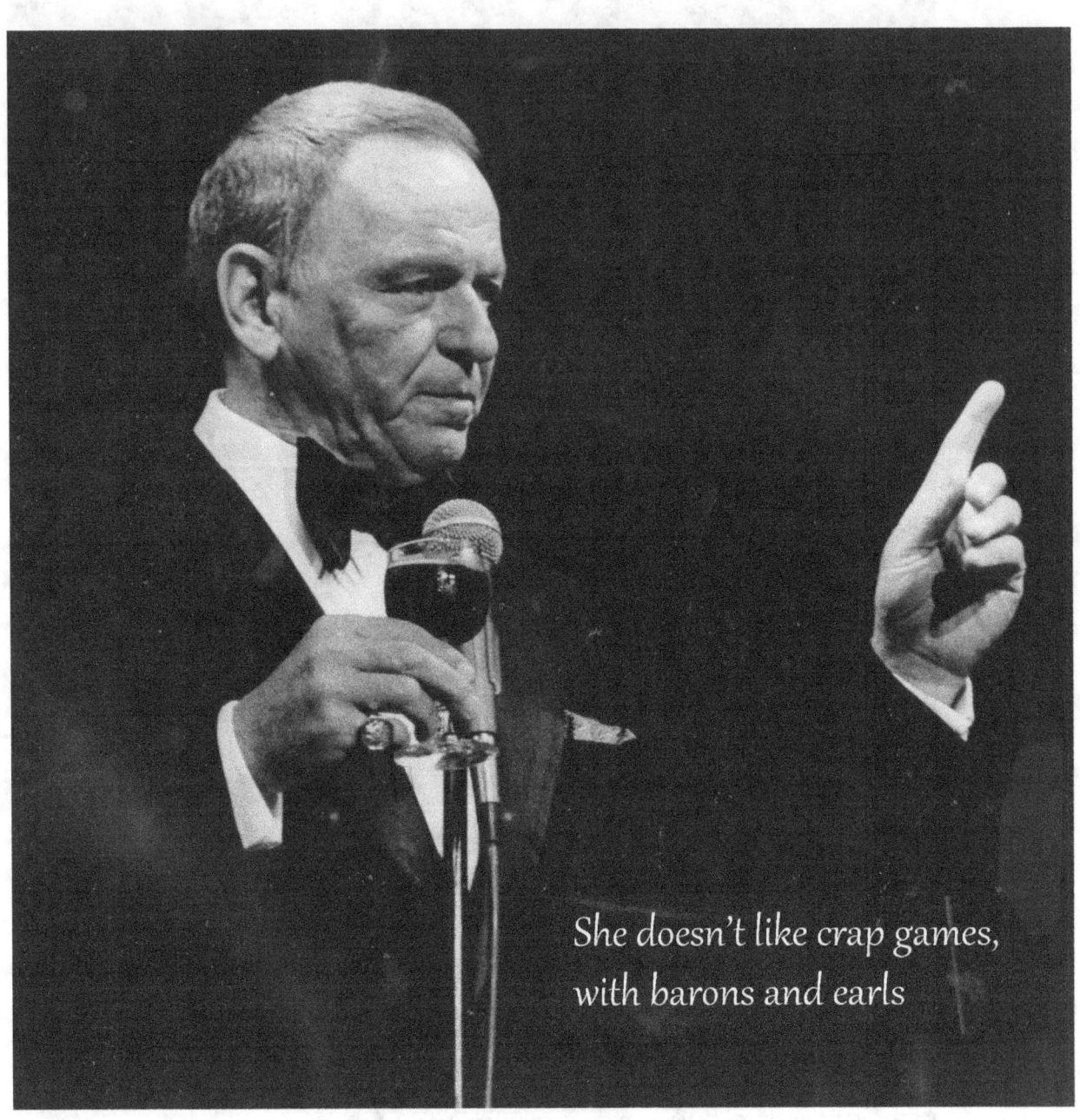

She doesn't like crap games,
with barons and earls

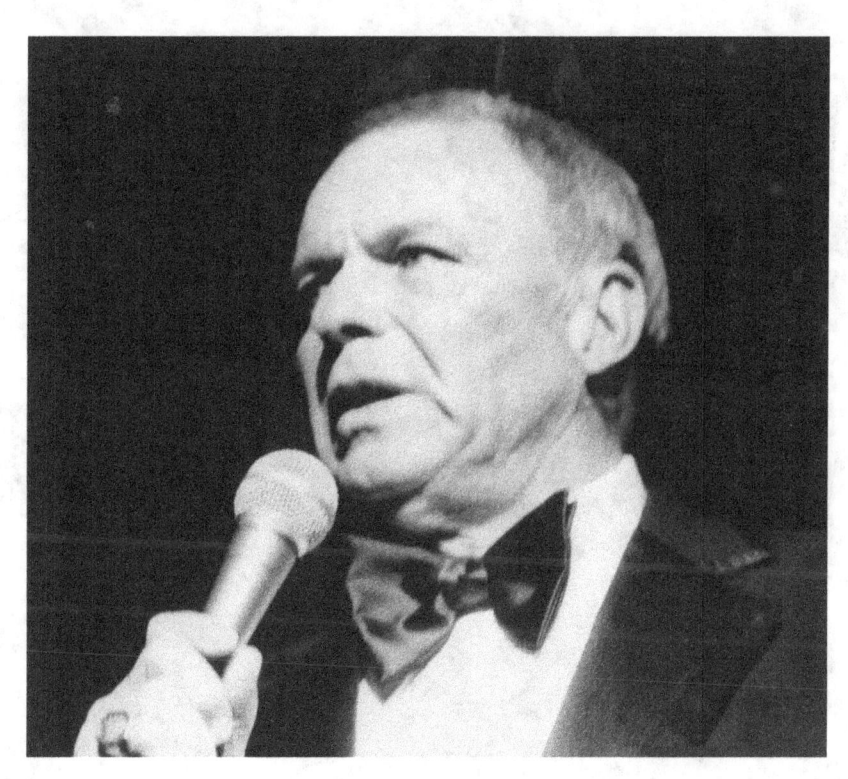

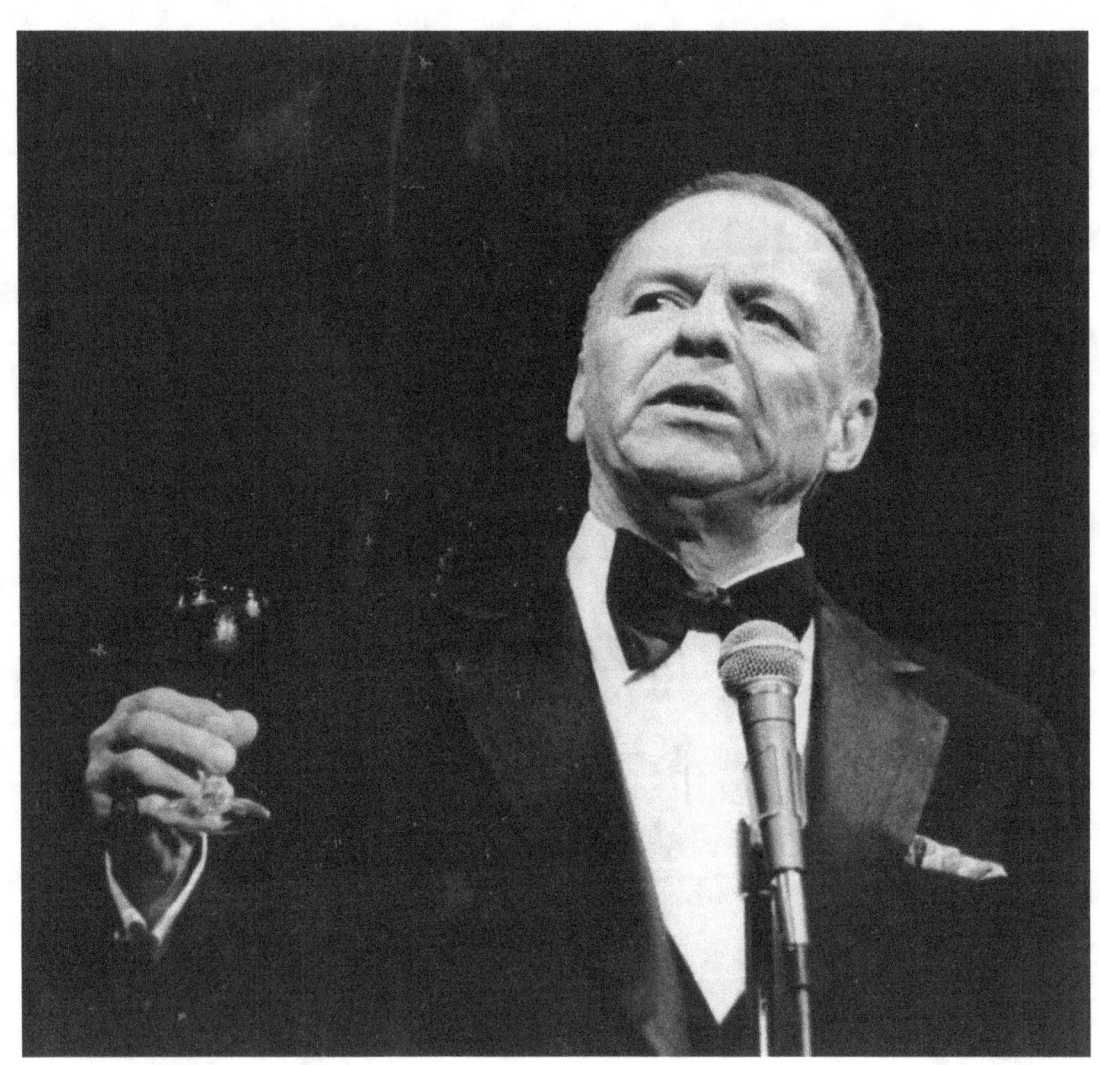

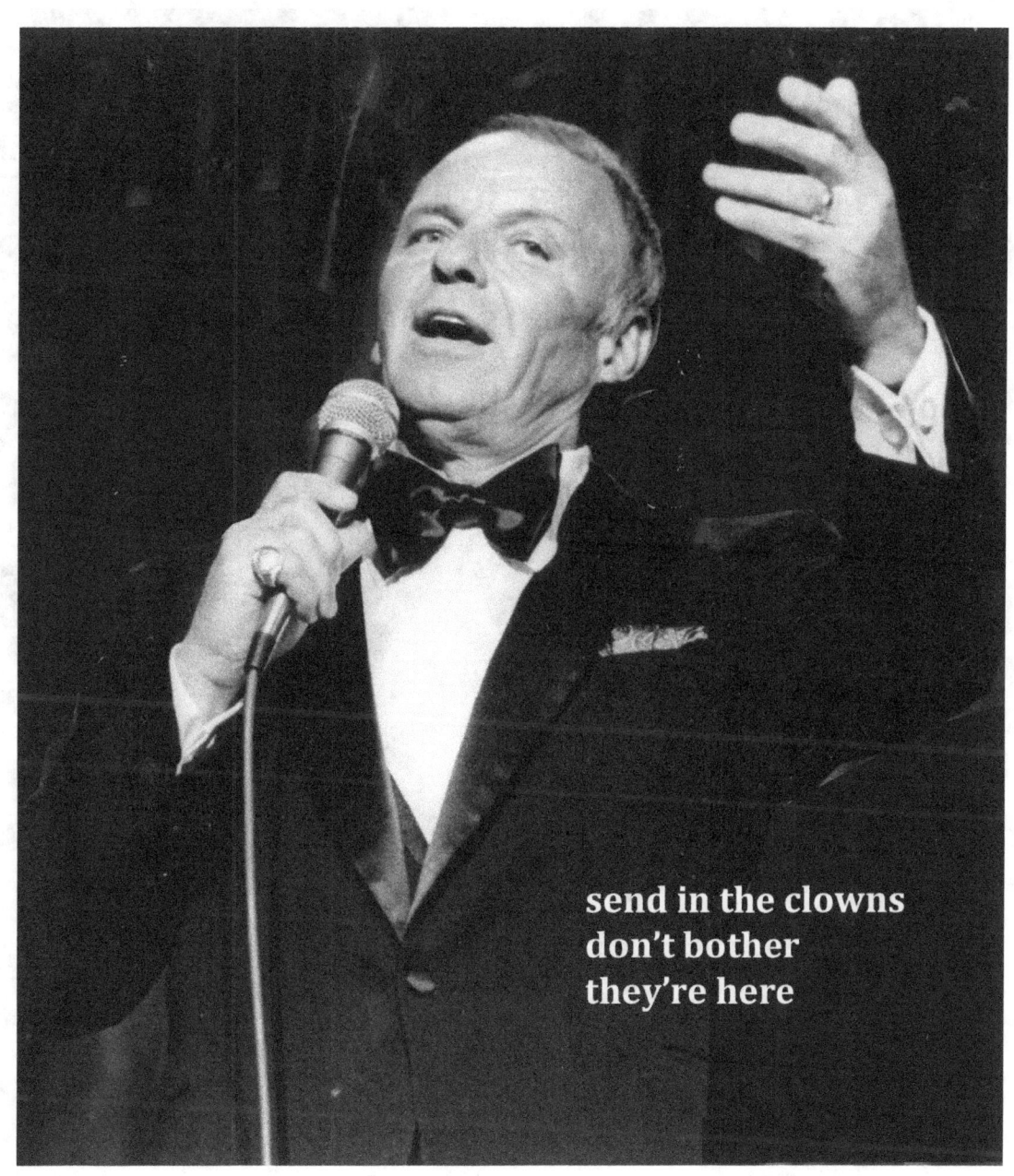

send in the clowns
don't bother
they're here

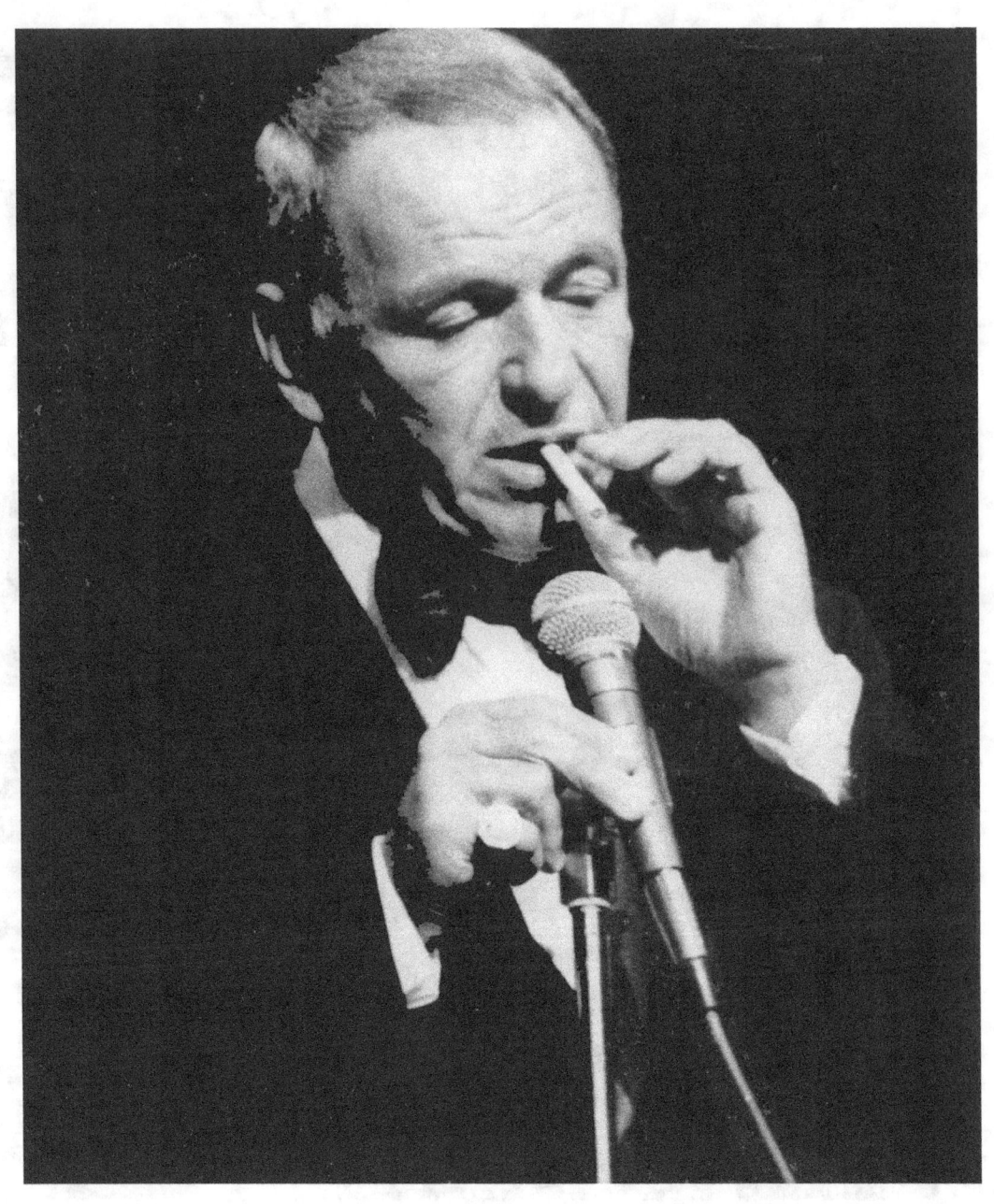

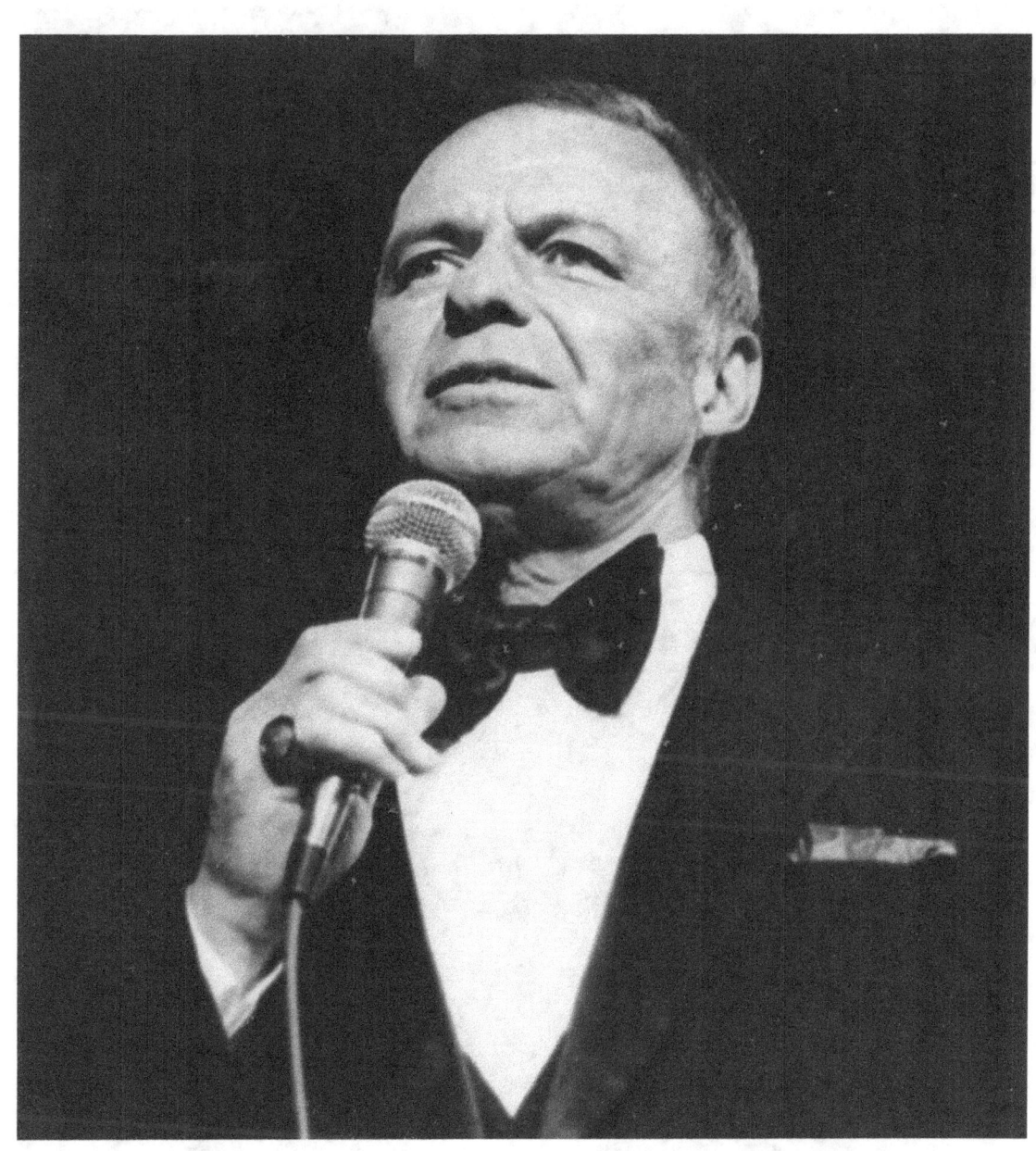

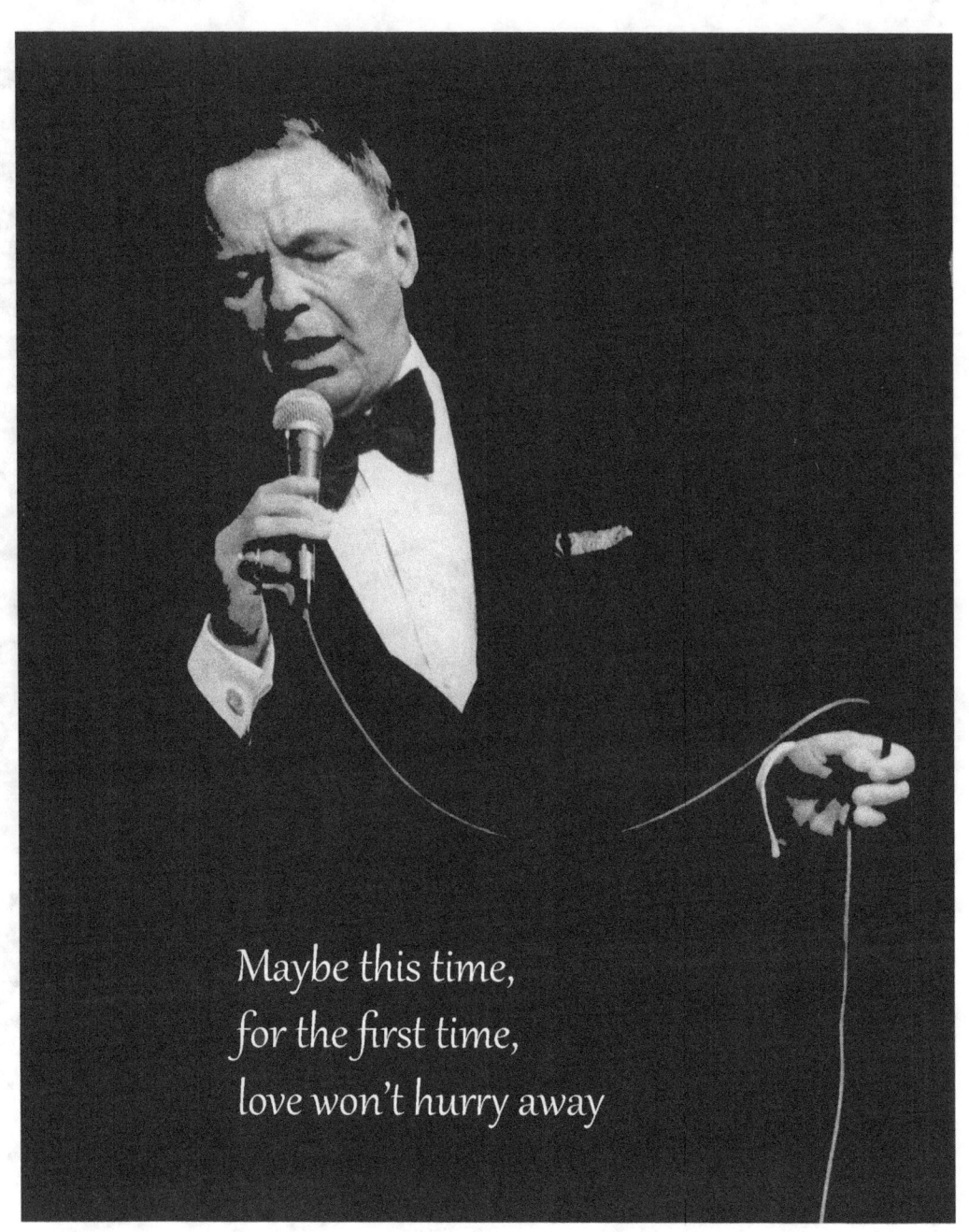

Maybe this time,
for the first time,
love won't hurry away

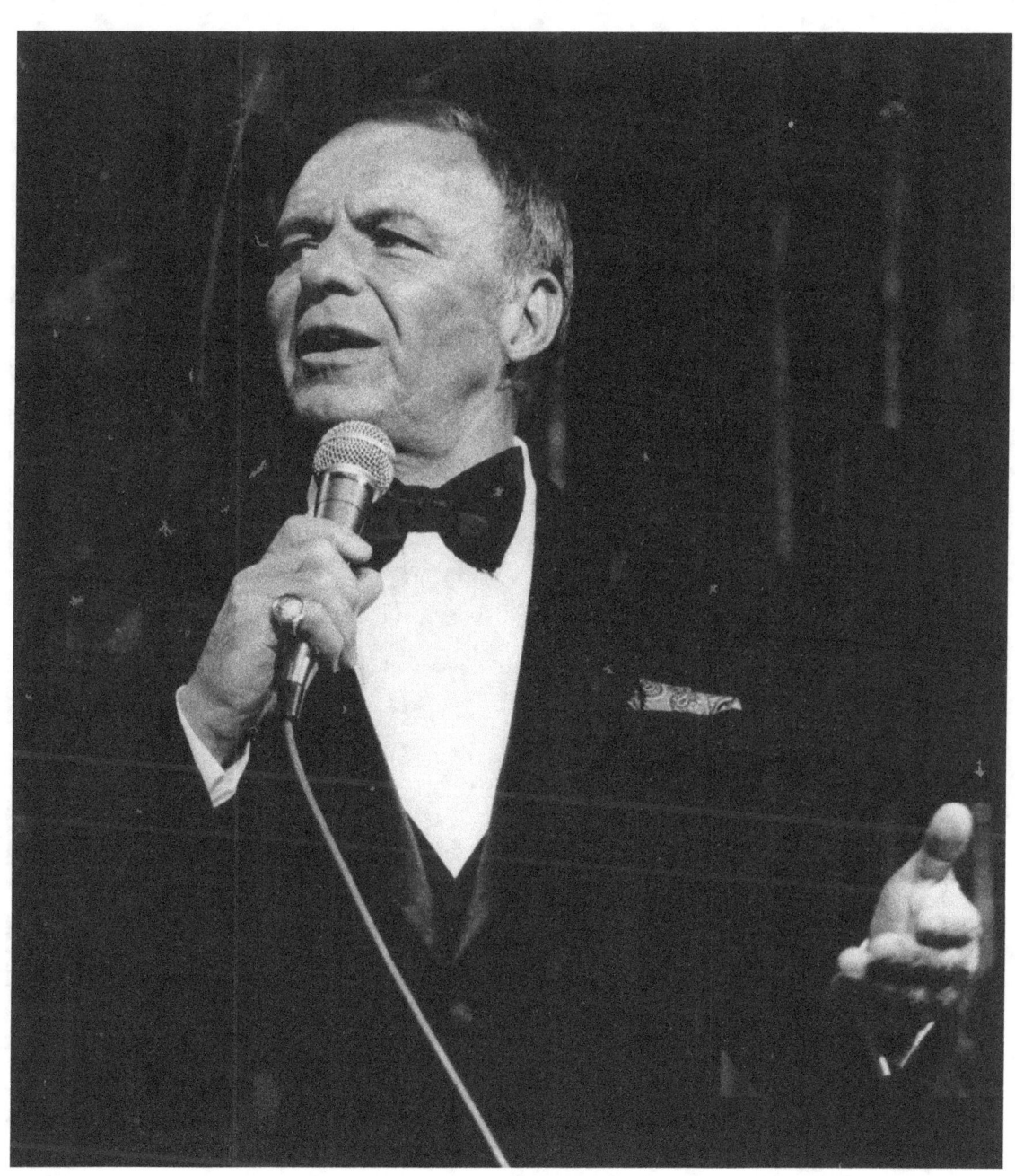

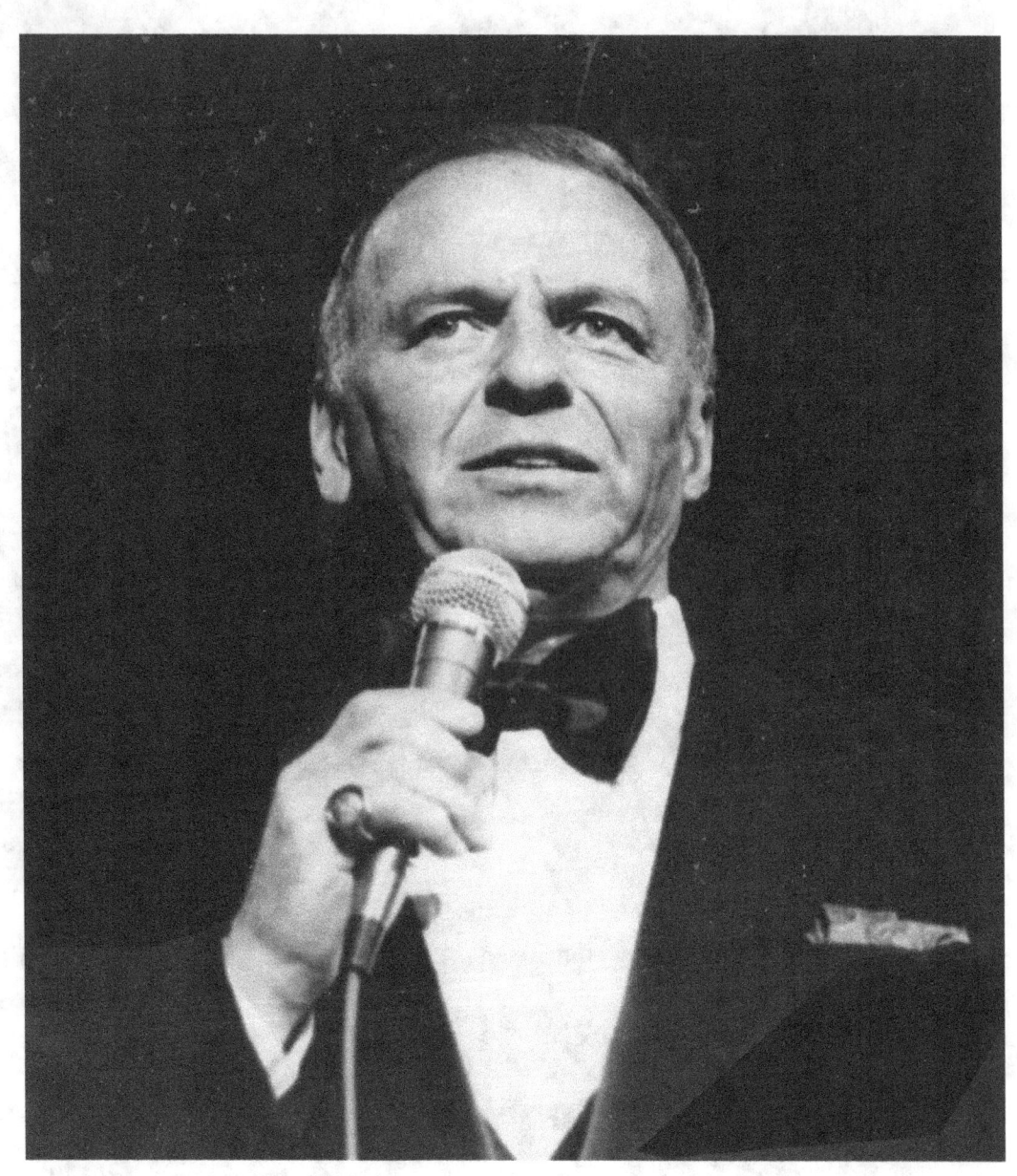

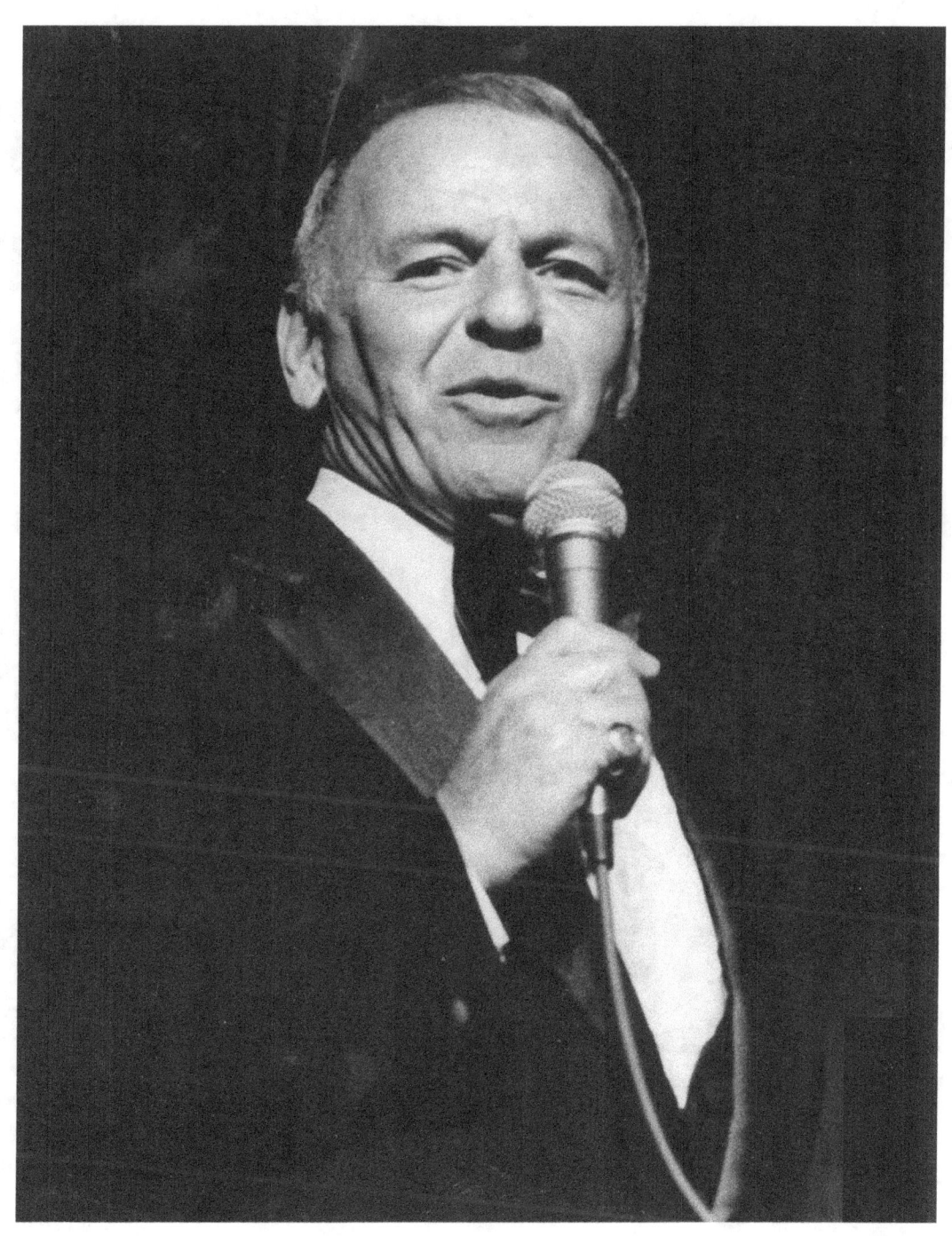

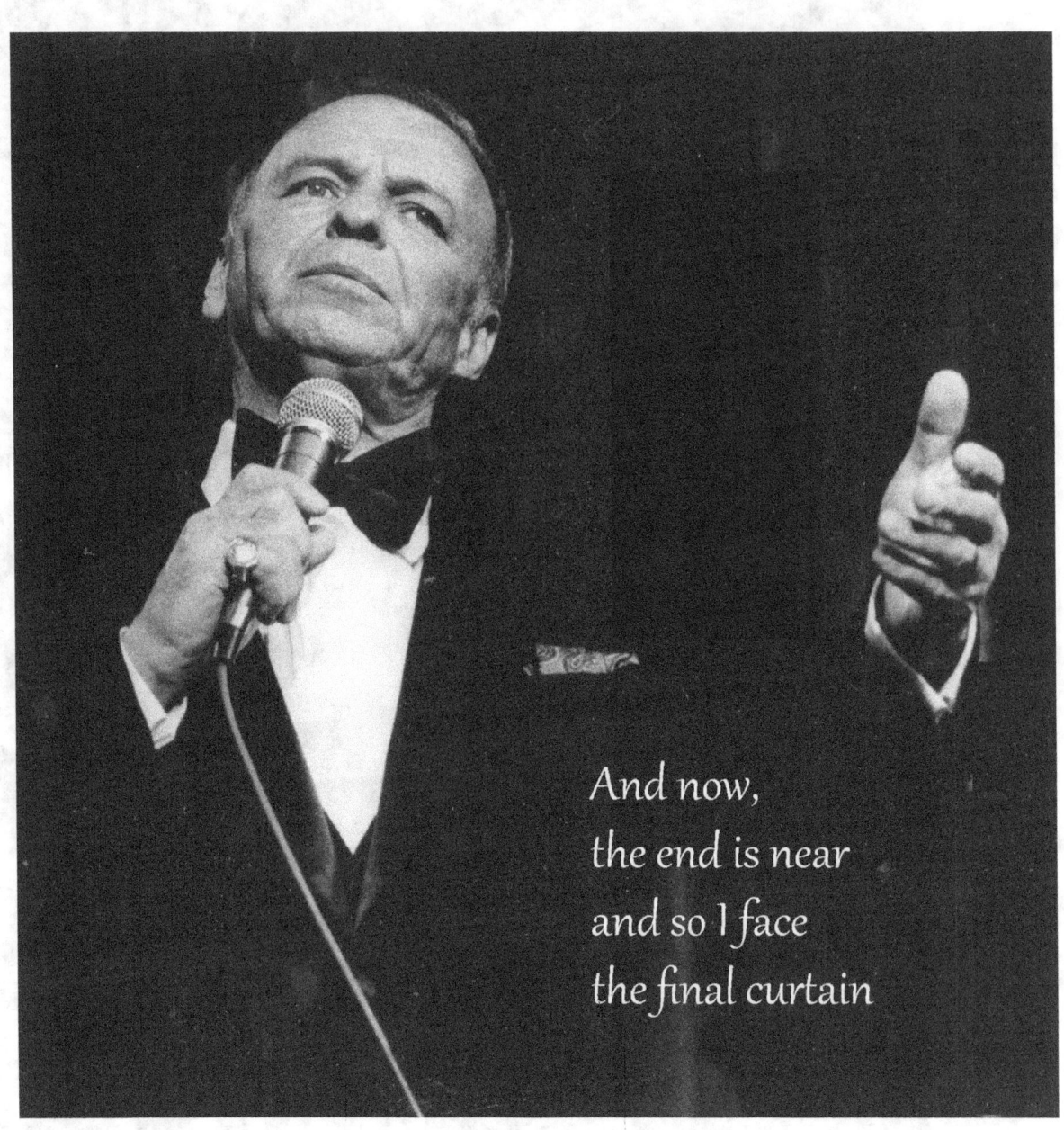

And now,
the end is near
and so I face
the final curtain

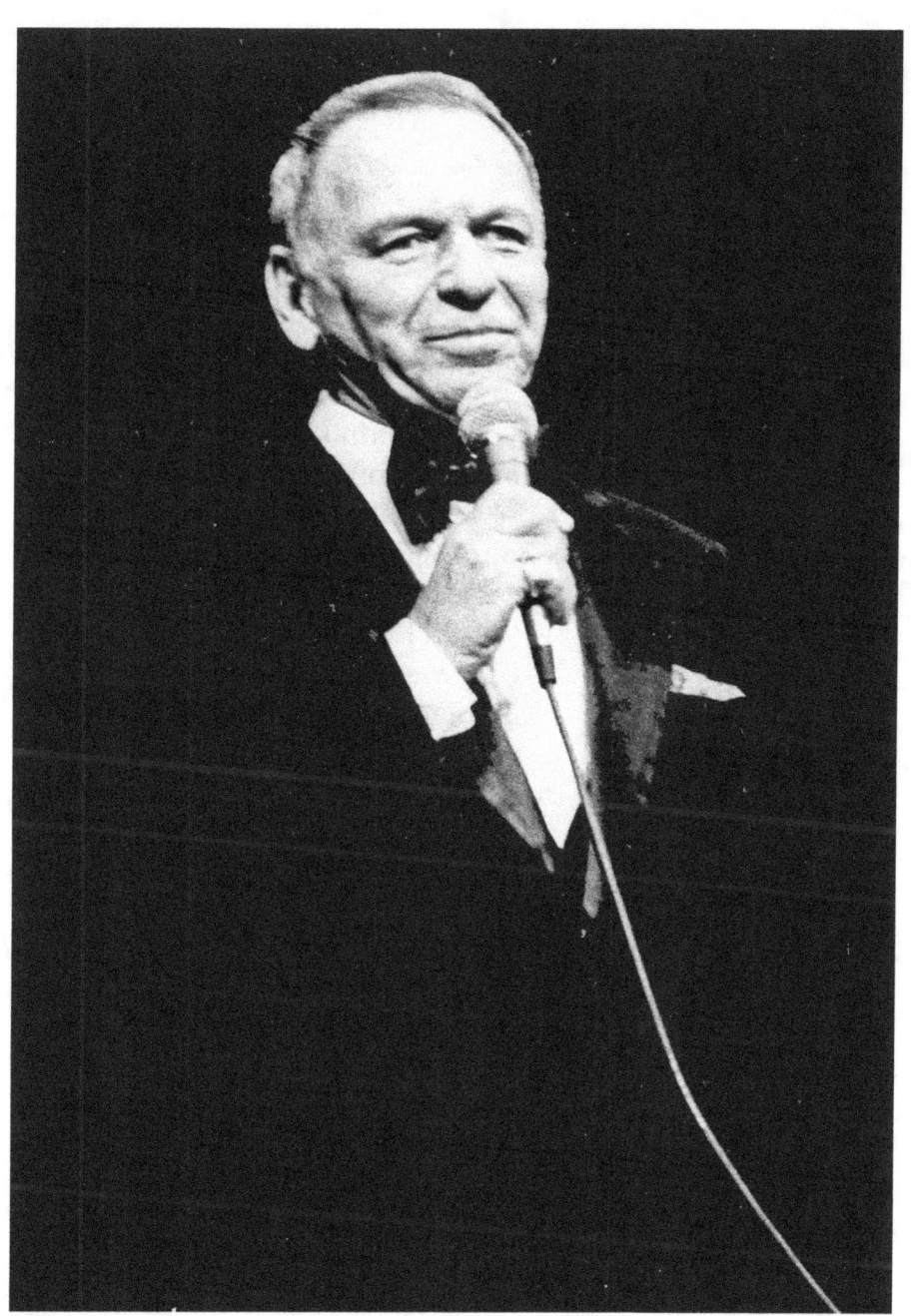

Frank's set list from May 26, 1978

1. All of Me
2. Maybe This Time
3. The Lady is a Tramp
4. Didn't We
5. Someone to Watch Over Me
6. Something
7. Baubles, Bangles and Beads
8. The Gal That Got Away
9. Remember
10. My Kind of Town
11. Send in the Clowns
12. Lonely Town
13. My Way
14. America the Beautiful

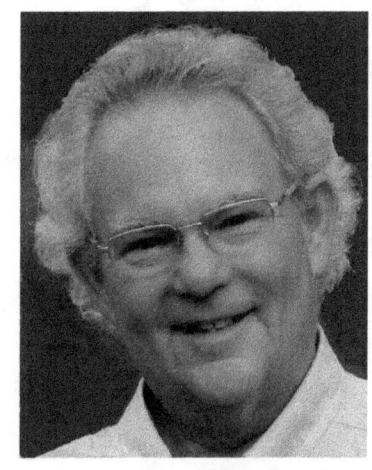

Lewis M. Weinstein

Lew Weinstein is an author
who lives with his wife Patricia Lenny
in Key West, FL.

He has published 4 novels ...
The Heretic
The Pope's Conspiracy
A Good Conviction
Case Closed

Mr. Weinstein's 5th novel,
A Flood of Evil,
will be published soon.